Dad's Toolbox

CeCe Wilson

Rosen Classroom
New York

A toolbox holds tools. It has special places for different tools. It is usually made of metal.

Workers use toolboxes at a job. They use the tools to build and repair things.

We also use toolboxes at home. We use tools for home improvement or repair. Dads and moms use tools to make things in the house work well.

My dad is a construction worker. He uses his toolbox at home and at work. He loves to show me his tools!

My dad shows me a hammer. He uses it to drive nails into a surface. Nails are in small compartments inside a toolbox.

My dad shows me pliers. Pliers are a tool for gripping. He uses them to turn bolts. He also uses them to bend wire.

My dad shows me a tape measure. He uses it to measure things. A good rule is to measure twice.

My dad shows me a screwdriver. He has different screwdrivers for different screws.

My dad shows me a saw. He uses it to cut wood. He uses his saw to build a birdhouse.

My dad shows me a helmet. He uses it to cover his head. My dad wears it at work for safety.

Words to Know

hammer

helmet

pliers

saw

screwdriver

toolbox